ESSENTIAL ELEMENTS®

GUITAR ENSEMBLES

CHRISTMAS CLASSICS

CONTENTS

Arrangements by Chip Henderson

ISBN 978-1-4584-1005-4

HAL•LEONARD®
CORPORATION

7777 W. BLUEMOUND RD. P.O. BOX 13819 MILWAUKEE, WI 53213

In Australia Contact:
Hal Leonard Australia Pty. Ltd.
4 Lentara Court
Cheltenham, Victoria, 3192 Australia
Email: ausadmin@halleonard.com.au

For all works contained herein:
Unauthorized copying, arranging, adapting, recording, Internet posting, public performance,
or other distribution of the printed music in this publication is an infringement of copyright.
Infringers are liable under the law.

Visit Hal Leonard Online at
www.halleonard.com

ANGELS FROM THE REALMS OF GLORY

Words by James Montgomery
Music by Henry T. Smart

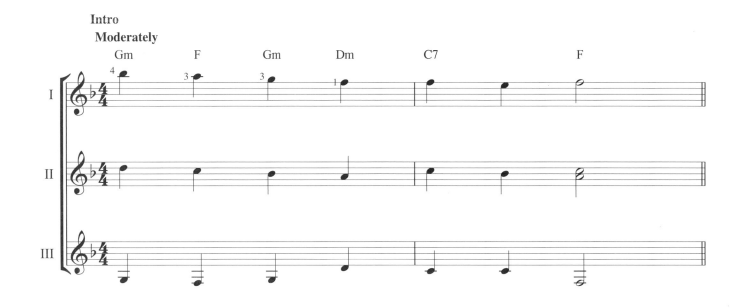

Copyright © 2011 by HAL LEONARD CORPORATION
International Copyright Secured   All Rights Reserved

ANGELS WE HAVE HEARD ON HIGH

Traditional French Carol
Translated by James Chadwick

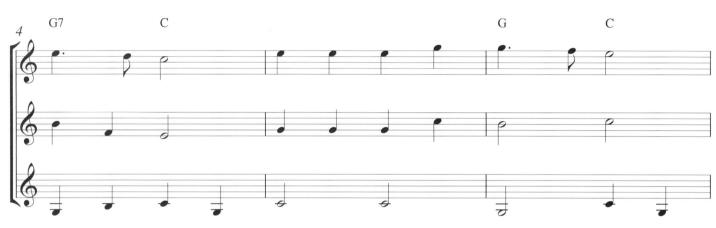

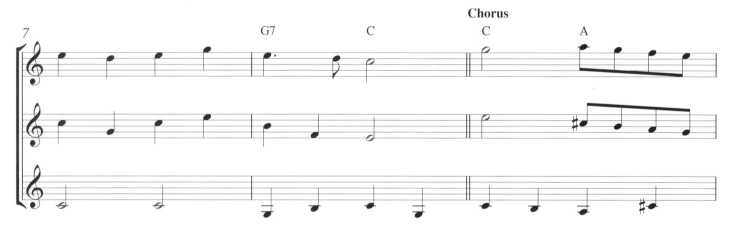

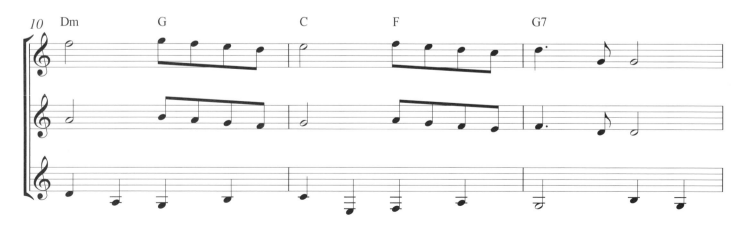

Copyright © 2011 by HAL LEONARD CORPORATION
International Copyright Secured   All Rights Reserved

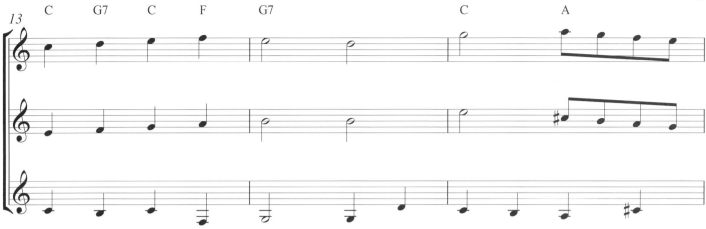

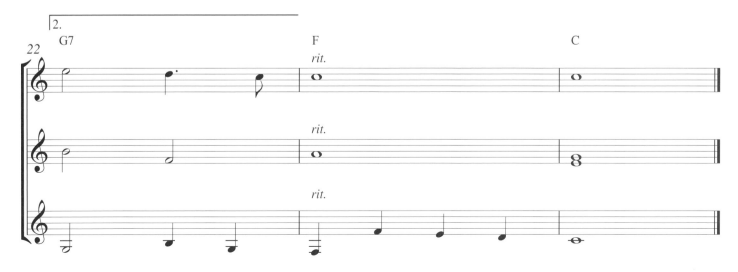

AWAY IN A MANGER

Words by John T. McFarland
Music by James R. Murray

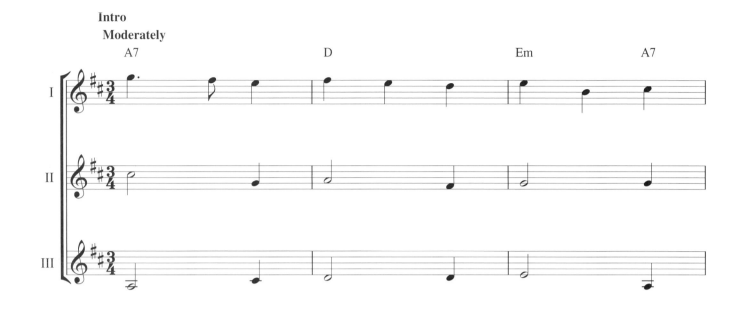

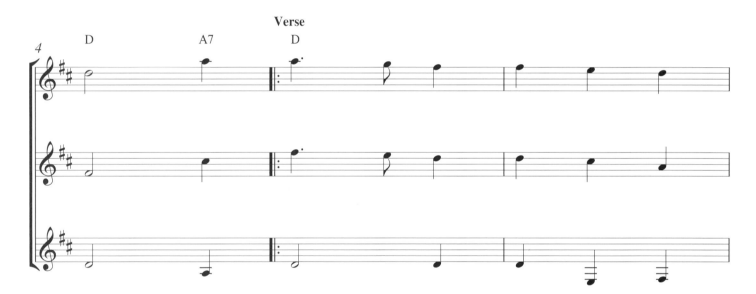

Copyright © 2011 by HAL LEONARD CORPORATION
International Copyright Secured   All Rights Reserved

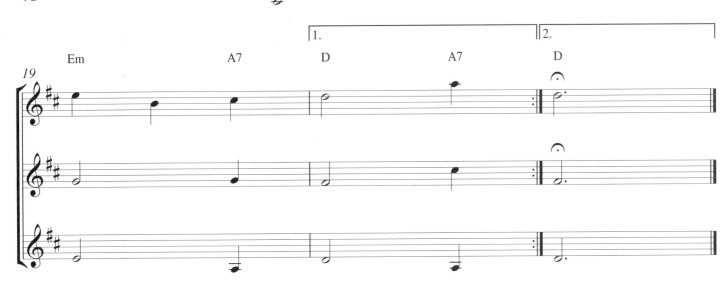

COVENTRY CAROL

Words by Robert Croo
Traditional English Melody

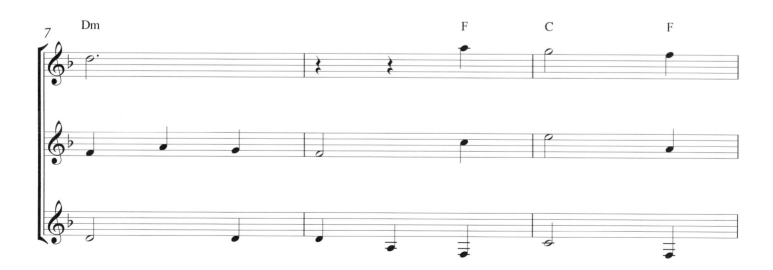

Copyright © 2011 by HAL LEONARD CORPORATION
International Copyright Secured   All Rights Reserved

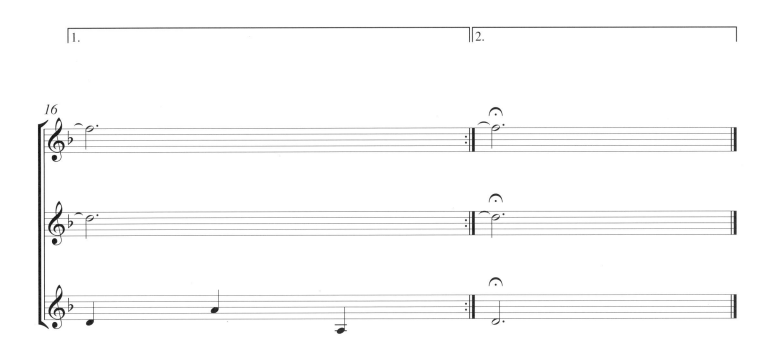

DECK THE HALL

Traditional Welsh Carol

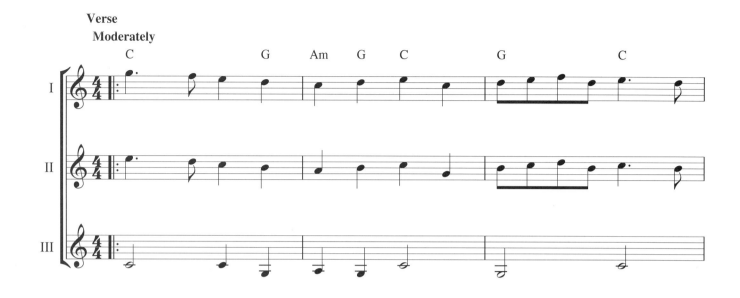

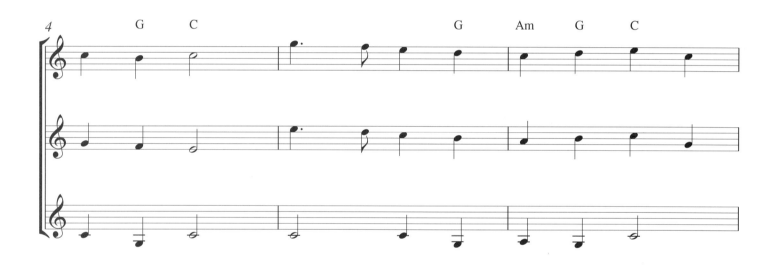

Copyright © 2011 by HAL LEONARD CORPORATION
International Copyright Secured   All Rights Reserved

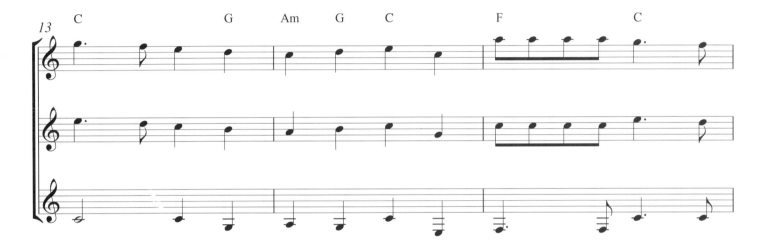

Outro

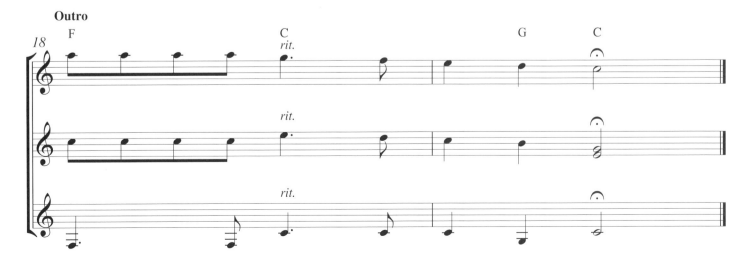

THE FIRST NOËL

17th Century English Carol
Music from W. Sandys' Christmas Carols

Verse
Moderately slow

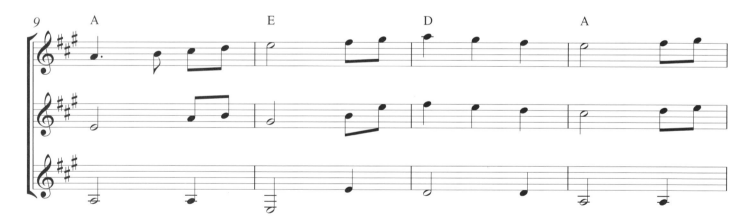

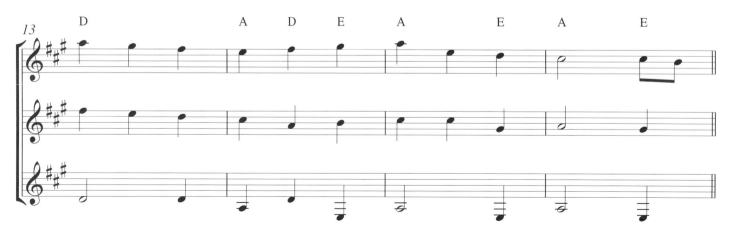

Copyright © 2011 by HAL LEONARD CORPORATION
International Copyright Secured   All Rights Reserved

Chorus

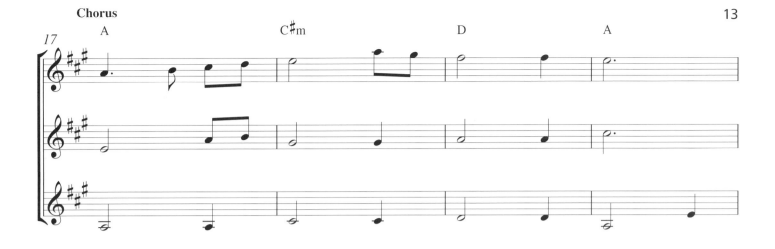

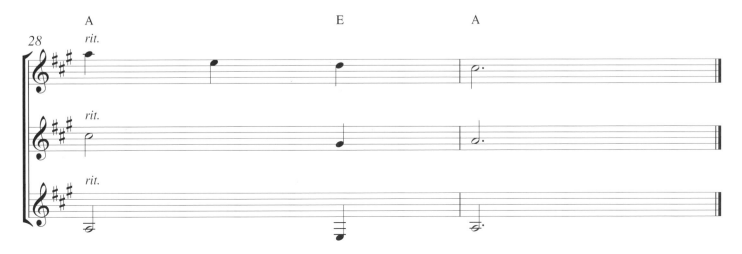

GOD REST YE MERRY, GENTLEMEN

19th Century English Carol

Verse

Moderately fast

Copyright © 2011 by HAL LEONARD CORPORATION
International Copyright Secured   All Rights Reserved

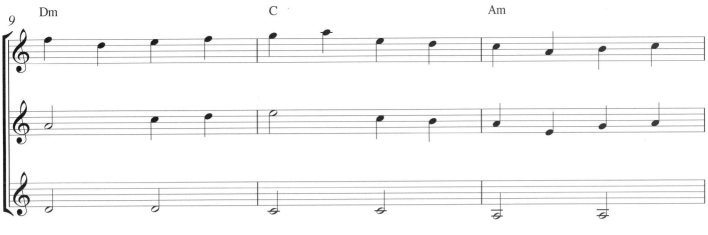

Chorus

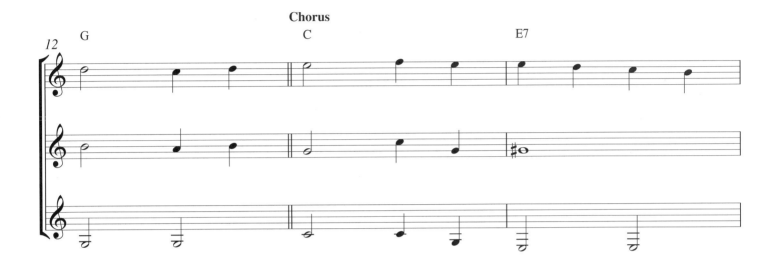

GOOD KING WENCESLAS

Words by John M. Neale
Music from Piae Cantiones

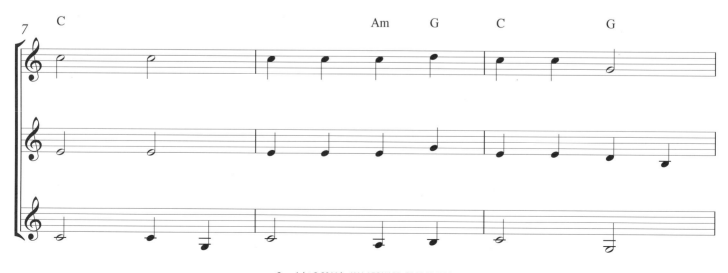

Copyright © 2011 by HAL LEONARD CORPORATION
International Copyright Secured   All Rights Reserved

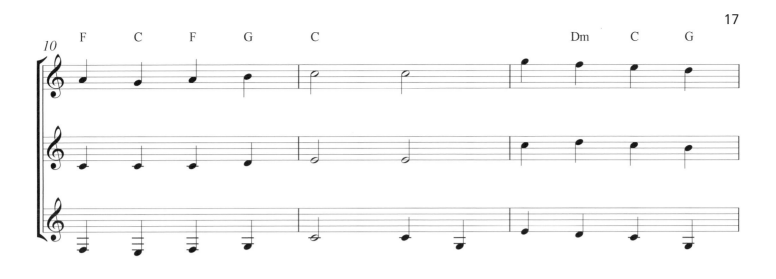

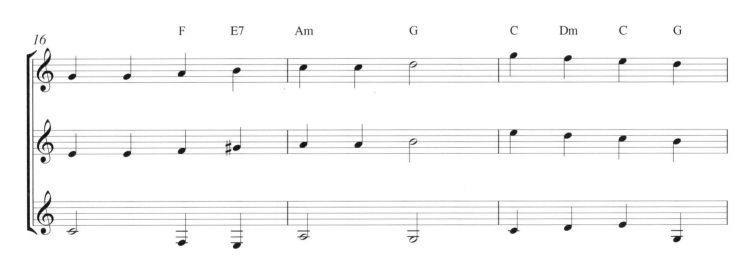

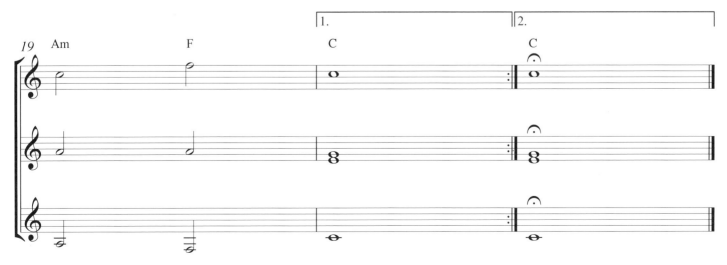

HARK! THE HERALD ANGELS SING

Words by Charles Wesley
Altered by George Whitefield
Music by Felix Mendelssohn-Bartholdy
Arranged by William H. Cummings

Copyright © 2011 by HAL LEONARD CORPORATION
International Copyright Secured   All Rights Reserved

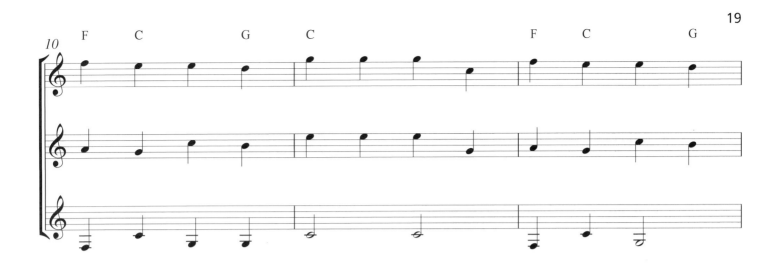

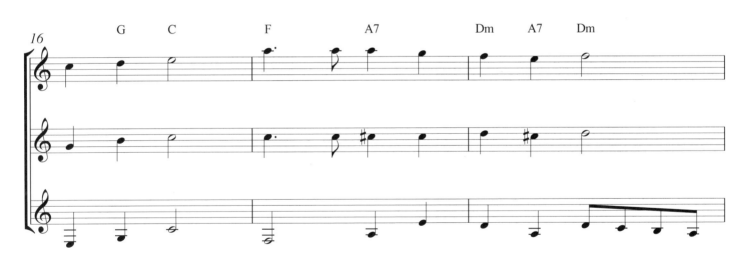

IT CAME UPON THE MIDNIGHT CLEAR

Words by Edmund Hamilton Sears
Music by Richard Storrs Willis

Verse
Moderately

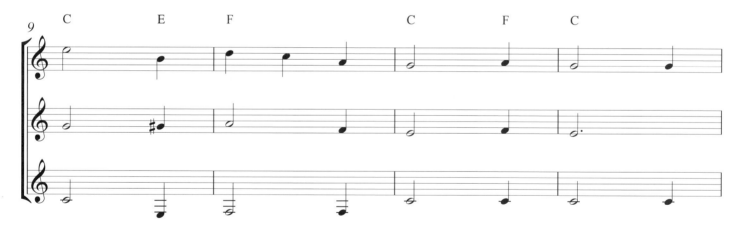

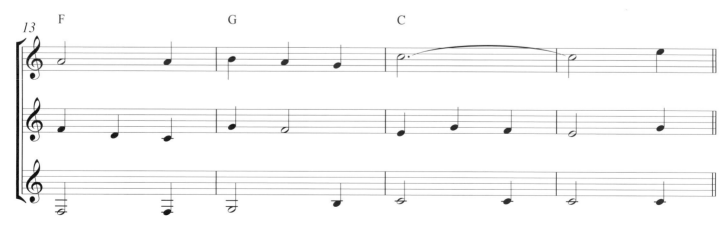

Copyright © 2011 by HAL LEONARD CORPORATION
International Copyright Secured   All Rights Reserved

Bridge

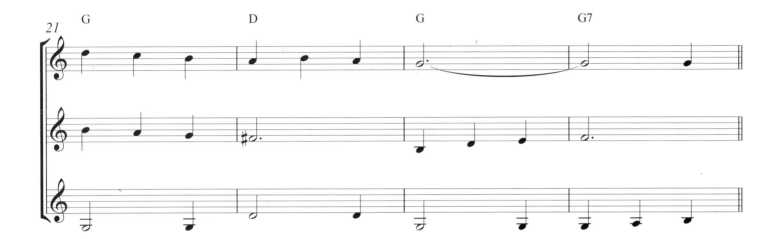

Verse

JINGLE BELLS

Words and Music by J. Pierpont

Copyright © 2011 by HAL LEONARD CORPORATION
International Copyright Secured   All Rights Reserved

Chorus

JOY TO THE WORLD

Words by Isaac Watts
Music by George Frideric Handel
Adapted by Lowell Mason

Verse
Moderately fast

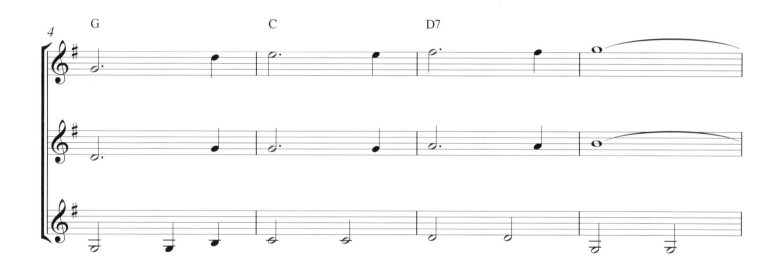

Copyright © 2011 by HAL LEONARD CORPORATION
International Copyright Secured   All Rights Reserved

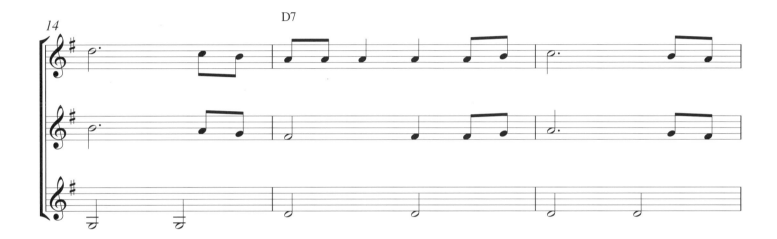

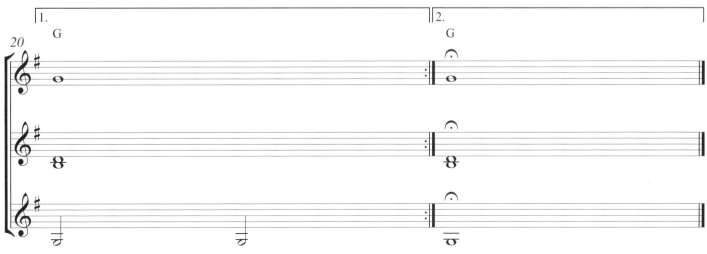

O COME, ALL YE FAITHFUL
(Adeste Fideles)

Music by John Francis Wade
Latin Words translated by Frederick Oakeley

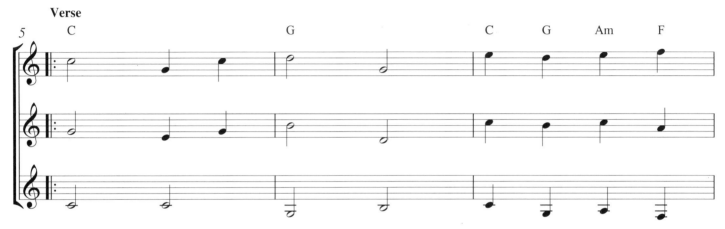

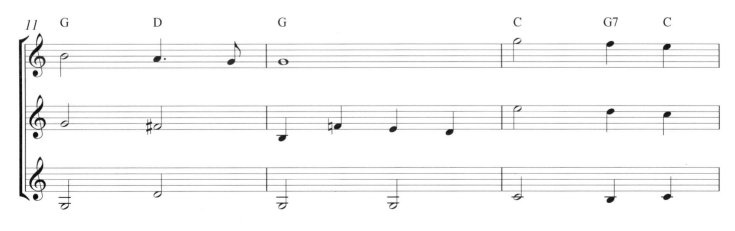

Copyright © 2011 by HAL LEONARD CORPORATION
International Copyright Secured   All Rights Reserved

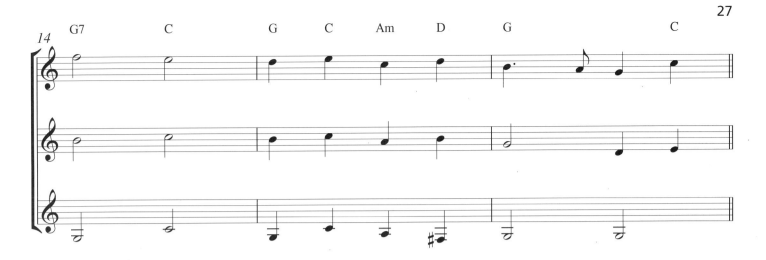

Chorus

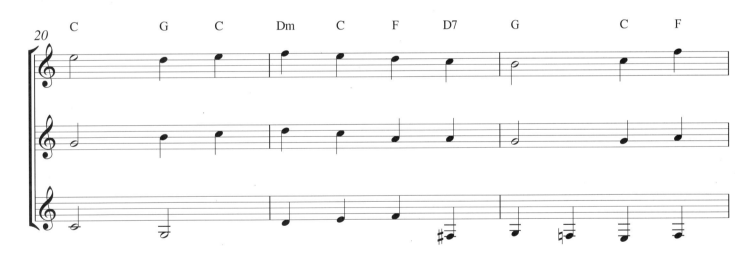

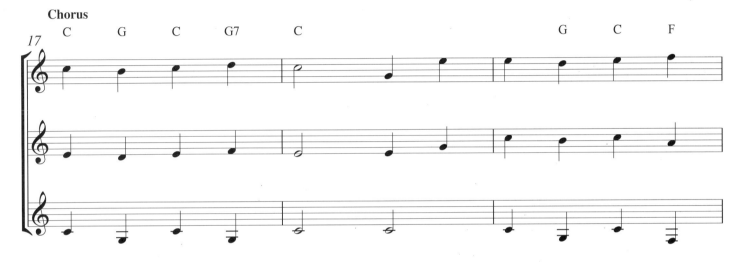

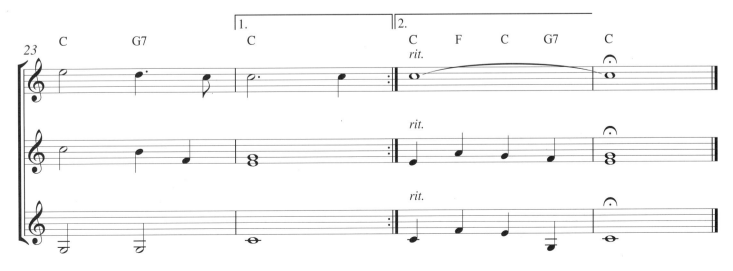

SILENT NIGHT

Words by Joseph Mohr
Translated by John F. Young
Music by Franz X. Gruber

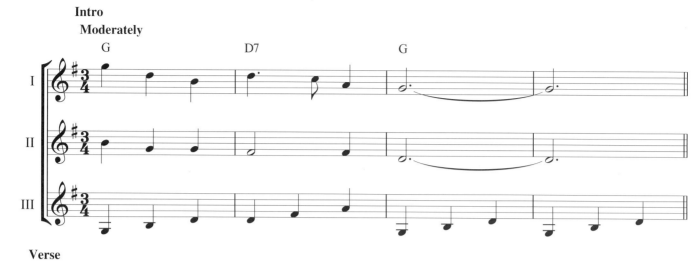

Copyright © 2011 by HAL LEONARD CORPORATION
International Copyright Secured   All Rights Reserved

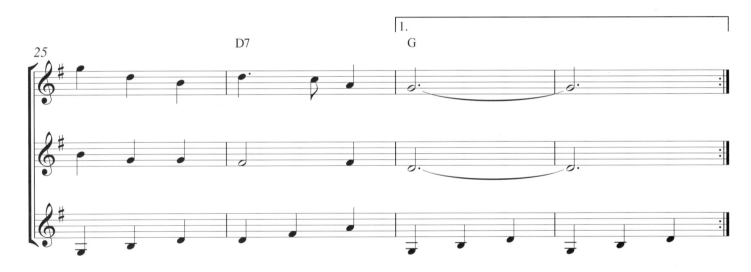

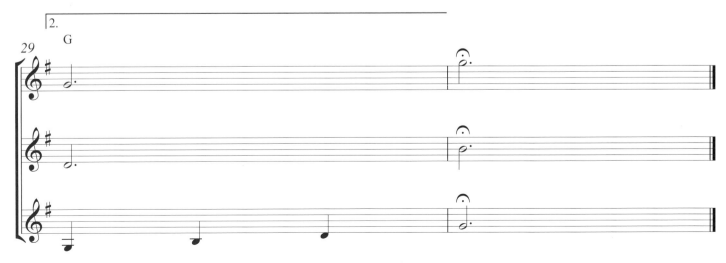

WE WISH YOU A MERRY CHRISTMAS

Traditional English Folksong

Copyright © 2011 by HAL LEONARD CORPORATION
International Copyright Secured   All Rights Reserved

⊕ Coda

ESSENTIAL ELEMENTS FOR GUITAR

Essential Elements Comprehensive Guitar Method

Take your guitar teaching to a new level! With popular songs in a variety of styles, and quality demonstration and backing tracks on the accompanying online audio, *Essential Elements for Guitar* is a staple of guitar teachers' instruction – and helps beginning guitar students off to a great start. This method was designed to meet the National Standards for Music Education, with features such as cross-curricular activities, quizzes, multicultural songs, basic improvisation and more.

BOOK 1

by Will Schmid and Bob Morris

Concepts covered in Book 1 include: getting started; basic music theory; guitar chords; notes on each string; music history; ensemble playing; performance spotlights; and much more! Songs include: Dust in the Wind • Eleanor Rigby • Every Breath You Take • Hey Jude • Hound Dog • Let It Be • Ode to Joy • Rock Around the Clock • Stand by Me • • Sweet Home Chicago • This Land Is Your Land • You Really Got Me • more!

00862639 Book/Online Audio $19.99
00001173 Book Only $14.99

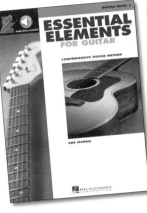

BOOK 2

by Bob Morris

Concepts taught in Book 2 include: playing melodically in positions up the neck; movable chord shapes up the neck; scales and extended chords in different keys; fingerpicking and pick style; improvisation in positions up the neck; and more! Songs include: Auld Lang Syne • Crazy Train • Folsom Prison Blues • La Bamba • Landslide • Nutcracker Suite • Sweet Home Alabama • Your Song • and more.

00865010 Book/Online Audio $22.99
00120873 Book Only $14.99

Essential Elements Guitar Ensembles

The songs in the Essential Elements Guitar Ensemble series are playable by three or more guitars. Each arrangement features the melody, a harmony part, and bass line in standard notation along with chord symbols. For groups with more than three or four guitars, the parts can be doubled. This series is perfect for classroom guitar ensembles or other group guitar settings.

Essential Elements Guitar Songs
INCLUDES TAB

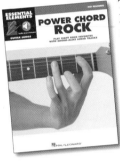

The books in the Essential Elements Guitar Songs series feature popular songs selected for the practice of specific guitar chord types. Each book includes eight songs and a CD with fantastic sounding play-along tracks. Practice at any tempo with the included Amazing Slow Downer software!

BARRE CHORD ROCK
00001137 Late-Beginner Level $12.99

POWER CHORD ROCK
00001139 Mid-Beginner Level $16.99

Mid-Beginner Level
EASY POP SONGS
00865011/$10.99

CHRISTMAS CLASSICS
00865015/$9.99

CHRISTMAS SONGS
00001136/$10.99

Late Beginner Level
CLASSICAL THEMES
00865005/$10.99

POP HITS
00001128/$12.99

ROCK CLASSICS
00865001/$10.99

Early Intermediate Level
J.S. BACH
00123103/$9.99

THE BEATLES
00172237/$12.99

CHRISTMAS FAVORITES
00128600/$12.99

DISNEY SONGS
00865014/$14.99

IRISH JIGS & REELS
00131525/$9.99

JAZZ BALLADS
00865002/$14.99

MULTICULTURAL SONGS
00160142/$9.99

POPULAR SONGS
00241053/$12.99

TOP SONGS 2010-2019
00295218/$9.99

Mid-Intermediate Level
THE BEATLES
00865008/$14.99

BOSSA NOVA
00865006/$12.99

CHRISTMAS CLASSICS
00865015/$9.99

DUKE ELLINGTON
00865009/$9.99

GREAT THEMES
00865012/$10.99

JIMI HENDRIX
00865013/$9.99

JAZZ STANDARDS
00865007/$14.99

ROCK HITS
00865017/$12.99

ROCK INSTRUMENTALS
00123102/$9.99

TOP HITS
00130606/$9.99

Late Intermediate to Advanced Level
JAZZ CLASSICS
00865016/$9.99

More Resources

DAILY GUITAR WARM-UPS
by Tom Kolb
Mid-Beginner to Late Intermediate
00865004 Book/Online Audio $14.99

GUITAR FLASH CARDS
96 Cards for Beginning Guitar
00865000.. $12.99

Prices, contents, and availability subject to change without notice.

www.halleonard.com